LIVE | DEAD

Live Dead is committed to planting churches among every unreached people group. We do so in teams that are multiagency, multinational, and multigenerational. Although Live Dead was started and is now stewarded by Assemblies of God World Missions (USA), we know and believe that Christ's commission is best obeyed in legitimate partnership with all the body of Christ.

Live Dead has three core values: Abiding (intimacy with Jesus through extravagant time in His presence reading the Bible and praying), Apostle (taking the gospel where the gospel has not gone, focusing on making disciples among all peoples and forming those disciples into indigenous churches), and Abandon (living a cruciform life by dying to self on a daily basis and paying any price to see Jesus glorified among all peoples).

Samuel Morris and the other missionaries that will be featured in future comic books lived out these values long before us, and we aim to follow in their steps with the empowering help of the Holy Spirit.

All the church must take all the gospel to all the world. God is calling men and women of every ethnicity and every age from every corner of the globe to represent Him among the nations.

If, after reading this comic book, your heart burns with passion to glorify Jesus among the unreached and you want to participate through giving, praying, going, or a combination of the three, visit livedead.org for more information.

Dick Brogden
United Arab Emirates, 2023

IN 1872, A PRINCE NAMED KABOO WAS BORN TO A TRIBAL CHIEF IN THE IVORY COAST.
IT WAS THE CUSTOM AT THE TIME THAT WHEN A TRIBE LOST A BATTLE, THE ELDEST SON OF THE CHIEF WAS TAKEN HOSTAGE UNTIL A RANSOM WAS PAID.
DURING HIS CHILDHOOD, KABOO WAS CAPTURED THREE TIMES.
THE FIRST TWO TIMES HE WAS RESCUED, BUT WHEN KABOO WAS 15, HIS TRIBE LOST AGAIN.
ONLY THIS TIME THERE WAS NO RESCUE.
KABOO'S TRIBE DID NOT COME FOR HIM.

HIS CAPTORS WERE LED BY A CRUEL MAN WHO WAS ALWAYS THINKING OF NEW WAYS TO TORTURE PEOPLE.
THEY PLANNED TO WHIP HIS BACK WITH A POISONOUS, THORNY VINE UNTIL HE BECAME TOO WEAK TO SIT OR STAND.
THEN THEY WOULD LAY HIM OVER A TREE TRUNK AND BEAT HIM UNTIL HE BECAME UNCONSCIOUS.
IF THAT DIDN'T KILL HIM, HIS TORTURERS WOULD THEN BURY HIM TO HIS NECK IN THE GROUND.
THEY PLANNED TO WEDGE HIS MOUTH OPEN WITH A STICK AND COAT IT WITH SOMETHING SWEET TO DRAW FLESH-EATING ANTS.
THE INSECTS WOULD BEGIN TO EAT THE SWEETNESS IN THE MOUTH ALONG WITH HIS FLESH, LEAVING HIS SKELETON AS A WARNING TO ALL WHO SAW IT.

BUT WHEN THEY PLACED KABOO ON THE TREE TO BEAT HIM, SOMETHING SUPERNATURAL OCCURRED, SOMETHING THAT ONLY THE EXISTENCE OF A POWERFUL GOD COULD EXPLAIN.
A BRIGHT LIGHT APPEARED AND COVERED HIM, AND A LOUD VOICE TOLD HIM TO RUN AWAY. THE VILLAGERS WHO WERE WATCHING EVEN HEARD THE VOICE.
AS THE VOICE SPOKE, KABOO GAINED A SUPERNATURAL STRENGTH. HE GOT UP AND RAN, EVENTUALLY STOPPING TO HIDE UNTIL NIGHT CAME.
AS THE SUN ROSE, A LIGHT BEGAN TO GUIDE HIM. HE FOLLOWED IT, THOUGH HE HAD NO IDEA WHERE IT WAS TAKING HIM.
HIS WEEKS-LONG JOURNEY TOOK HIM THROUGH A TROPICAL FOREST FILLED WITH CANNIBALS, WILD ANIMALS, AND POISONOUS SNAKES, BUT HE WAS KEPT SAFE.
HE FOUND PLENTY OF FRUITS AND NUTS TO EAT ALONG THE WAY.

EVENTUALLY, KABOO CAME UPON A PLANTATION OUTSIDE MONROVIA, THE CAPITAL OF LIBERIA.
THE DAY KABOO ESCAPED AND THE DAY HE ARRIVED WERE BOTH FRIDAYS, SO EVERY FRIDAY FROM THE DAY HE ARRIVED AT THE PLANTATION, HE FASTED FOOD AND DRINK IN REMEMBRANCE OF HIS STORY AND BEGAN TO CALL FRIDAY HIS "DELIVERANCE DAY."
THAT FIRST SUNDAY IN THE CITY, KABOO VISITED A CHURCH WHERE HE HEARD A MISSIONARY SPEAKER TELL THE STORY OF PAUL.
WHEN THE MISSIONARY MENTIONED THE BRIGHT LIGHT ON THE DAMASCUS ROAD, KABOO JUMPED UP AND EXCLAIMED:
"I HAVE SEEN THAT LIGHT. IT IS THE SAME LIGHT THAT BROUGHT ME HERE!"
KABOO STARTED FOLLOWING JESUS.

KABOO SOON REALIZED HOW MUCH MORE HE NEEDED TO GROW IN HIS NEWFOUND FAITH.
HE WANTED REVENGE ON THOSE WHO HAD TORTURED HIM, BUT HE ALSO WANTED MORE OF GOD AND TO BE FREE FROM FEAR.
AFTER LONG DAYS OF WORK AT THE PLANTATION, HE SPENT HOURS IN PRAYER.
HIS ROOMMATES DID NOT UNDERSTAND HIS LONGING FOR GOD, SO HE RETREATED INTO THE WOODS TO PRAY.

LATE ONE NIGHT HE RETURNED TO HIS BED WHILE HIS HEART WAS STILL IN A PLACE OF PRAYER. HE LATER DESCRIBED IT THIS WAY:
"ALL AT ONCE MY ROOM GREW LIGHT. AT FIRST, I THOUGHT THE SUN WAS RISING, BUT THE OTHERS WERE SOUND ASLEEP. THE ROOM GREW LIGHTER, UNTIL IT WAS FILLED WITH GLORY."
"THE BURDEN OF MY HEART SUDDENLY DISAPPEARED, AND I WAS FILLED WITH A SENSE OF INNER JOY. MY BODY FELT AS LIGHT AS A FEATHER."
"I WAS FILLED WITH A POWER THAT MADE ME FEEL I COULD ALMOST FLY. I COULD NOT CONTAIN MY JOY, BUT SHOUTED UNTIL EVERYONE IN THE BARRACKS WAS AWAKENED."
"I'M THE SON OF THE HEAVENLY KING!"
"I WAS NOW A SON OF THE HEAVENLY KING. I KNEW THEN THAT MY FATHER HAD SAVED ME FOR A PURPOSE AND THAT HE WOULD WORK WITH ME."

HE DID NOT UNDERSTAND THE THEOLOGY OF WHAT HAD JUST HAPPENED, BUT THROUGH HIS DEEP LONGING FOR GOD, HIS TOTAL TRUST IN HIM, AND A CHILDLIKE FAITH, THE HOLY SPIRIT CAME TO HIM.
GOD HAD ANSWERED HIS PRAYERS FOR CLOSENESS AND POWER.
KABOO WAS BAPTIZED IN THE METHODIST CHURCH OF MONROVIA AND TOOK THE NAME SAMUEL MORRIS.

IN MONROVIA, HE MET A SLAVE FROM THE TRIBE THAT CAPTURED HIM.
THE SLAVE WITNESSED SAMUEL'S ESCAPE. HE ALSO SAW THE BRIGHT LIGHT AND HEARD THE VOICE TELLING SAMUEL TO RUN.
SAMUEL SHARED THE GOSPEL WITH HIM, AND HE WAS LATER BAPTIZED AND GIVEN THE NAME HENRY O'NEIL.
HENRY AND SAMUEL BECAME GREAT FRIENDS AND FAITHFUL SERVANTS OF JESUS.
LATER, SAMUEL BEGAN TO SEARCH FOR INFORMATION ABOUT THE HOLY SPIRIT, TALKING WITH EVERY MISSIONARY HE COULD FIND.
FINALLY, WHEN ONE FRIEND WAS UNABLE TO ANSWER HIS QUESTIONS ANY FURTHER, SHE TOLD HIM THAT EVERYTHING SHE KNEW ABOUT THE HOLY SPIRIT CAME FROM STEPHEN MERRITT IN NEW YORK CITY.
SAMUEL SAID,
I WILL GO TO NEW YORK TO SEE HIM.

SAMUEL BEGAN TO LOOK FOR A NEW YORK-BOUND SHIP AND FOUND A CAPTAIN BARGAINING OVER CARGO.
SAMUEL WALKED UP TO THE CAPTAIN AND DECLARED,
MY FATHER IN HEAVEN TOLD ME YOU WOULD TAKE ME TO NEW YORK. I WANT TO SEE STEPHEN MERRITT WHO LIVES THERE.
YOU'RE CRAZY, BOY.
SAID THE CAPTAIN BEFORE WALKING AWAY.
AFTER THAT, SAMUEL RETURNED TO THE BEACH SEVERAL TIMES TO REPEAT HIS DECLARATION.
EVENTUALLY, THE CAPTAIN FOUND HIMSELF SHORT CREW MEMBERS, AND SAMUEL CAME UP AND ANNOUNCED,
MY FATHER TOLD ME YOU WILL TAKE ME NOW.
THE CAPTAIN ASKED HOW MUCH HE SHOULD PAY SAMUEL, AND SAMUEL RESPONDED, "NOTHING. JUST TAKE ME TO NEW YORK, SO I CAN SEE STEPHEN MERRITT."

AS SAMUEL BOARDED THE BOAT, HE NOTICED A YOUNG MAN ON DECK WHO COULD NOT WALK AFTER AN INJURY.
HE STOPPED AND PRAYED FOR HIM, AND IMMEDIATELY GOD HEALED HIM.
THE CAPTAIN SOON REALIZED THAT SAMUEL KNEW NOTHING ABOUT SHIPS.
HE WAS ABOUT TO SEND HIM TO SHORE WHEN THE YOUNG MAN WHO WAS HEALED PLEADED SAMUEL'S CASE,
PLEASE KEEP HIM. HE HAS DONE SO MUCH FOR ME.
THE CAPTAIN ALLOWED SAMUEL TO STAY BUT DID NOT SPARE HIM AN OCCASIONAL BEATING.

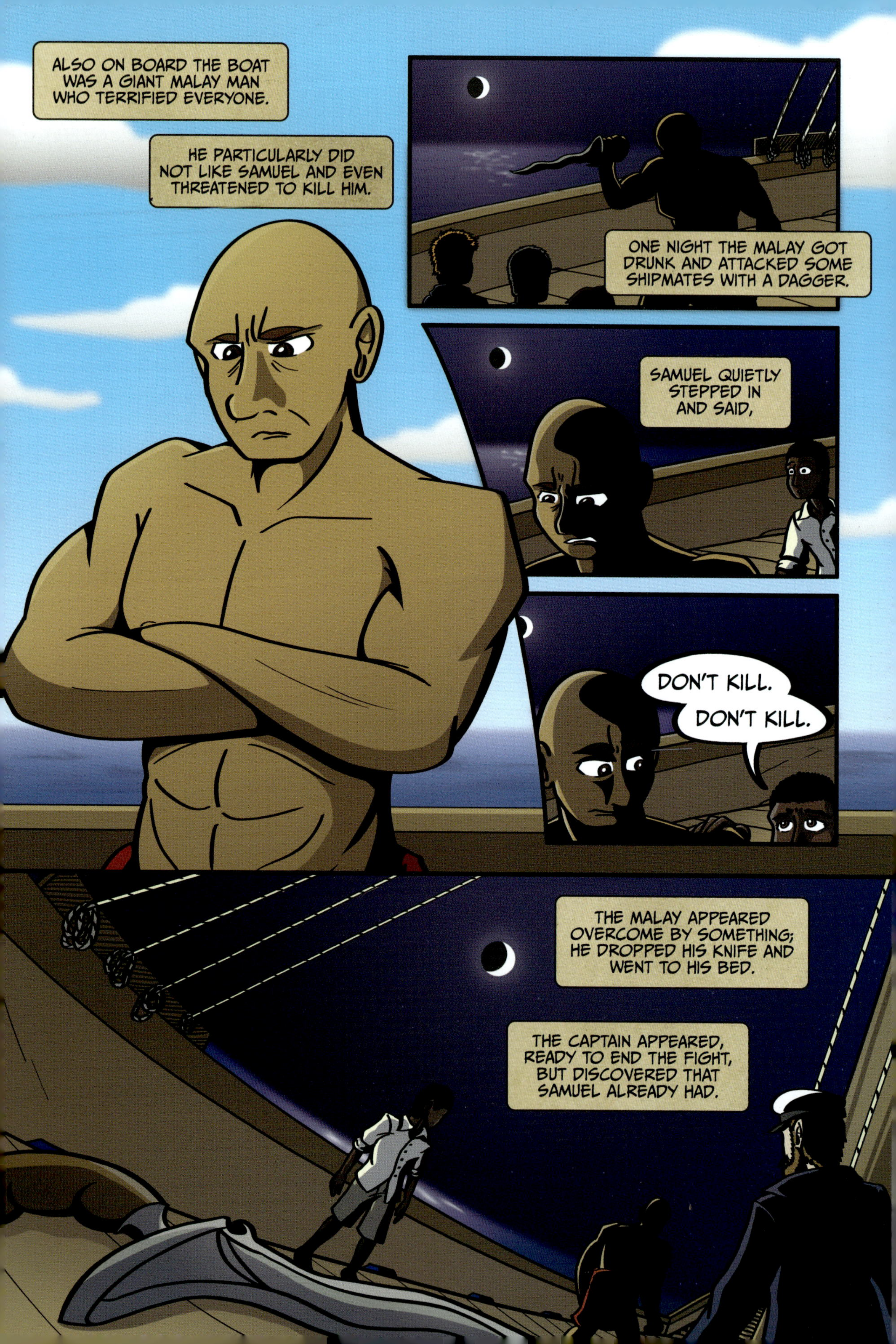
ALSO ON BOARD THE BOAT WAS A GIANT MALAY MAN WHO TERRIFIED EVERYONE.
HE PARTICULARLY DID NOT LIKE SAMUEL AND EVEN THREATENED TO KILL HIM.
ONE NIGHT THE MALAY GOT DRUNK AND ATTACKED SOME SHIPMATES WITH A DAGGER.
SAMUEL QUIETLY STEPPED IN AND SAID,
DON'T KILL.
DON'T KILL.
THE MALAY APPEARED OVERCOME BY SOMETHING; HE DROPPED HIS KNIFE AND WENT TO HIS BED.
THE CAPTAIN APPEARED, READY TO END THE FIGHT, BUT DISCOVERED THAT SAMUEL ALREADY HAD.

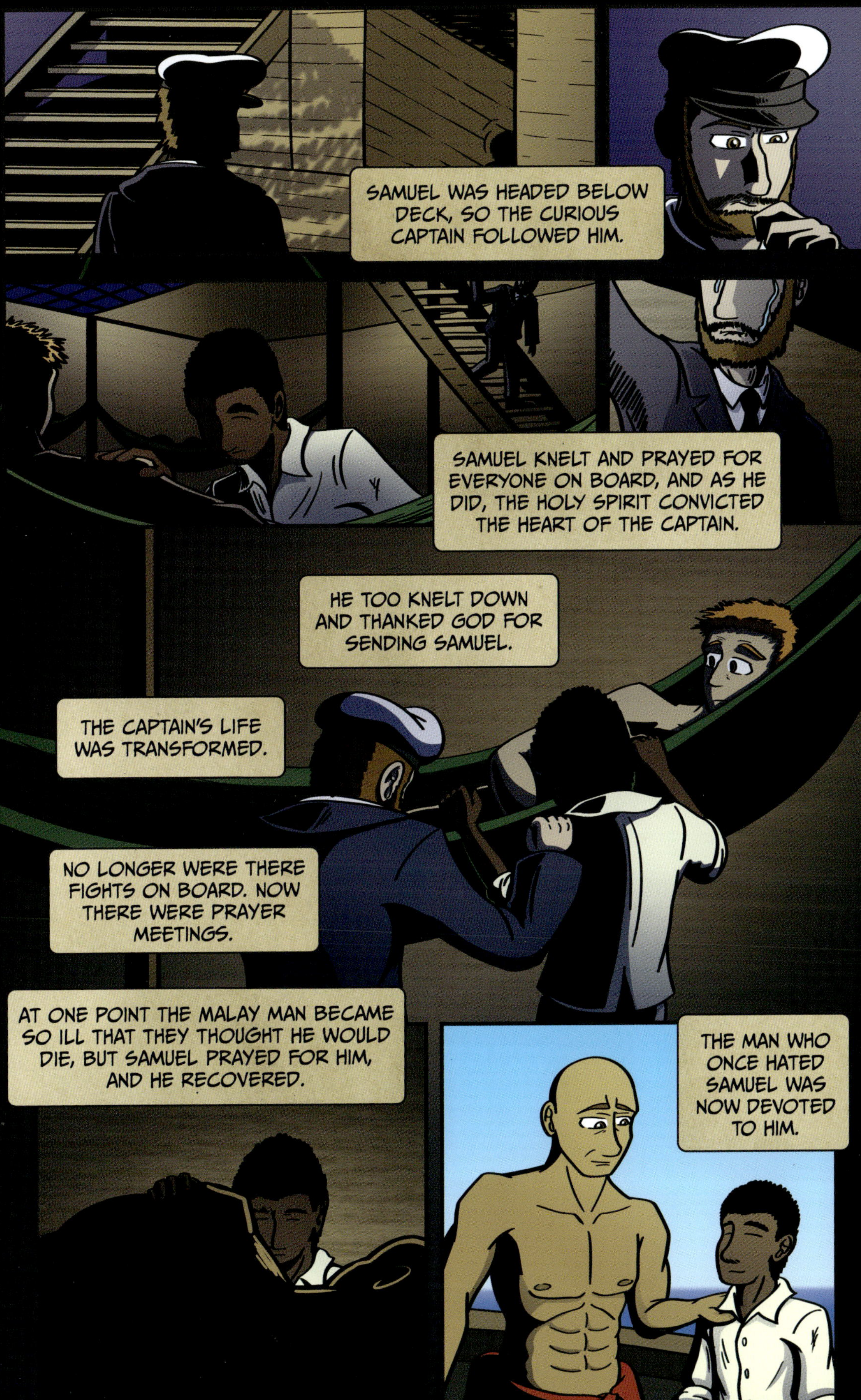
SAMUEL WAS HEADED BELOW DECK, SO THE CURIOUS CAPTAIN FOLLOWED HIM.
SAMUEL KNELT AND PRAYED FOR EVERYONE ON BOARD, AND AS HE DID, THE HOLY SPIRIT CONVICTED THE HEART OF THE CAPTAIN.
HE TOO KNELT DOWN AND THANKED GOD FOR SENDING SAMUEL.
THE CAPTAIN'S LIFE WAS TRANSFORMED.
NO LONGER WERE THERE FIGHTS ON BOARD. NOW THERE WERE PRAYER MEETINGS.
AT ONE POINT THE MALAY MAN BECAME SO ILL THAT THEY THOUGHT HE WOULD DIE, BUT SAMUEL PRAYED FOR HIM, AND HE RECOVERED.
THE MAN WHO ONCE HATED SAMUEL WAS NOW DEVOTED TO HIM.

WHEN THEY ARRIVED IN NEW YORK AFTER SIX MONTHS AT SEA, THE SHIP'S CREW SADLY SAID GOOD BYE TO SAMUEL.
THEY HAD BECOME FRIENDS ON THE VOYAGE AND SAMUEL'S GODLY INFLUENCE HAD LED SOME TO FOLLOW JESUS.
THE SHIP ARRIVED ON A FRIDAY, SAMUEL'S "DELIVERANCE DAY."

$1 IN THE 1890S HAS THE APPROXIMATE VALUE OF $32 IN 2023.

N
WHEN HE RETURNED LATER, MR. MERRITT FOUND SAMUEL SURROUNDED BY SEVENTEEN MEN AT THE MISSION.
HIS FACE GLOWED WITH GOD'S LIGHT AS THE MEN KNEELED AND WEPT FOR GOD'S MERCY.
MR. MERRITT BROUGHT SAMUEL TO HIS HOME AND GAVE HIM THE SPECIAL GUEST ROOM.
LIFE IN NEW YORK WAS SO DIFFERENT FROM HIS LIFE EXPERIENCES UP UNTIL THAT POINT, BUT MR. AND MRS. MERRITT WERE HAPPY TO HELP HIM ADJUST.

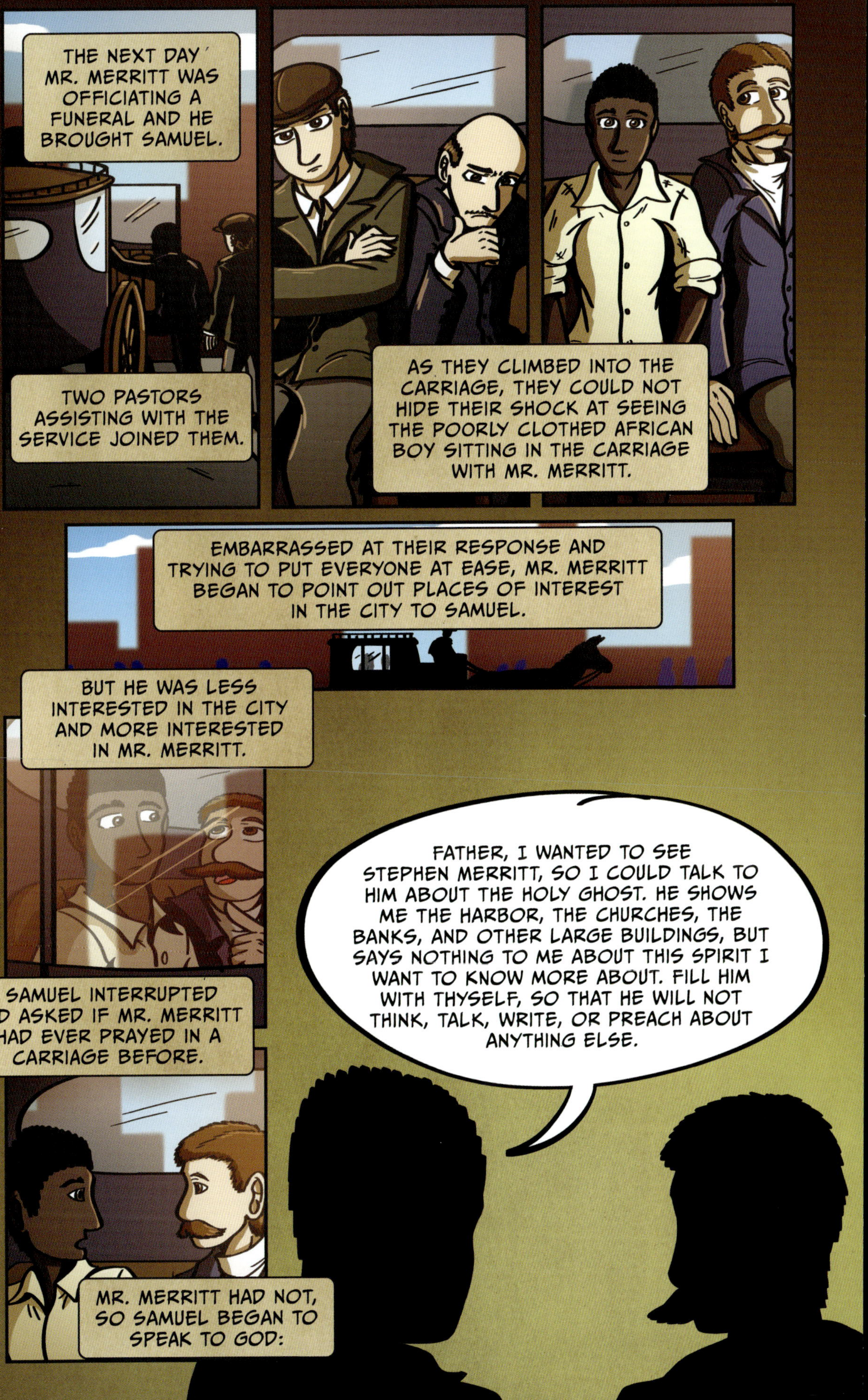
THE NEXT DAY MR. MERRITT WAS OFFICIATING A FUNERAL AND HE BROUGHT SAMUEL.
TWO PASTORS ASSISTING WITH THE SERVICE JOINED THEM.
AS THEY CLIMBED INTO THE CARRIAGE, THEY COULD NOT HIDE THEIR SHOCK AT SEEING THE POORLY CLOTHED AFRICAN BOY SITTING IN THE CARRIAGE WITH MR. MERRITT.
EMBARRASSED AT THEIR RESPONSE AND TRYING TO PUT EVERYONE AT EASE, MR. MERRITT BEGAN TO POINT OUT PLACES OF INTEREST IN THE CITY TO SAMUEL.
BUT HE WAS LESS INTERESTED IN THE CITY AND MORE INTERESTED IN MR. MERRITT.
SAMUEL INTERRUPTED AND ASKED IF MR. MERRITT HAD EVER PRAYED IN A CARRIAGE BEFORE.
MR. MERRITT HAD NOT, SO SAMUEL BEGAN TO SPEAK TO GOD:
FATHER, I WANTED TO SEE STEPHEN MERRITT, SO I COULD TALK TO HIM ABOUT THE HOLY GHOST. HE SHOWS ME THE HARBOR, THE CHURCHES, THE BANKS, AND OTHER LARGE BUILDINGS, BUT SAYS NOTHING TO ME ABOUT THIS SPIRIT I WANT TO KNOW MORE ABOUT. FILL HIM WITH THYSELF, SO THAT HE WILL NOT THINK, TALK, WRITE, OR PREACH ABOUT ANYTHING ELSE.

NEVER IN HIS LIFE AS A MINISTER HAD THE PRESENCE OF THE HOLY SPIRIT FELT SO REAL TO STEPHEN MERRITT AS IN THAT MOMENT WHEN SAMUEL PRAYED.
SAMUEL WAS IN LOVE WITH HIS GOD. FROM THAT MOMENT MR. MERRITT'S LIFE WAS NEVER THE SAME.
EVEN HIS FRIENDS IN THE MINISTRY SAW A HOLINESS IN HIM THAT THEY HAD NEVER SEEN BEFORE.
THE FUNERAL SERVICE THAT DAY WAS ONE OF THE BEST SERMONS MR. MERRITT EVER GAVE. THE MOVE OF THE HOLY SPIRIT WAS SO POWERFUL THAT THE CASKET BECAME AN ALTAR FOR REPENTANCE.

MR. MERRITT KNEW SAMUEL CAME TO AMERICA TO LEARN MORE ABOUT GOD AND HE BELIEVED THAT SAMUEL COULD RECEIVE THE BEST CHRISTIAN EDUCATION AT TAYLOR UNIVERSITY.
HE SENT HIS RECOMMENDATION TO THE SCHOOL, CALLING SAMUEL A "DIAMOND IN THE ROUGH."
ON A SUNDAY, SAMUEL JOINED MR. MERRITT AT A SUNDAY SCHOOL AND WAS INVITED TO TALK ABOUT THE HOLY SPIRIT.
THE MORE EDUCATED PEOPLE IN THE ROOM FOUND THE SIGHT OF SAMUEL ON THE PLATFORM AMUSING UNTIL HE BEGAN TO SPEAK.
AS HE SHARED, THE PRESENCE OF GOD SWEPT THROUGH THE ROOM AND THOSE IN THE ROOM WERE MOVED TO TEARS.
AS A RESULT THEY CREATED THE SAMUEL MORRIS MISSIONARY SOCIETY TO GATHER THE CLOTHING, BOOKS, AND OTHER ITEMS HE NEEDED FOR COLLEGE. THEY COLLECTED THREE TRUNKS WORTH.

SAMUEL ARRIVED IN FORT WAYNE, INDIANA ON A FRIDAY, HIS "DELIVERANCE DAY."
DR. READE, THE COLLEGE PRESIDENT, ASKED SAMUEL IF HE HAD ANY PREFERENCE ABOUT WHERE HE WOULD LIVE.
IF THERE IS A ROOM NOBODY ELSE WANTS, GIVE IT TO ME.
DR. READE WAS MOVED BY SAMUEL'S RESPONSE. HE WROTE TO A FRIEND:
I turned away, for my eyes were full of tears. I was asking myself whether I was willing to take what nobody else wanted.
In my experience as a teacher, I have had occasion to assign rooms to more than a thousand students. Most of them were noble Christian young ladies and gentlemen,
but Sammy Morris was the only one of them who ever said, "If there is a room nobody else wants, give it to me."
THE COLLEGE STRUGGLED FINANCIALLY, BUT THEY DESIRED THAT SAMUEL RECEIVE HIS EDUCATION.
AN APPEAL FOR MONEY WAS MADE TO LITTLE RESPONSE, UNTIL JOSIAH KICHLER, A LOCAL BUTCHER, GAVE FIVE DOLLARS FOR WHAT HE CALLED THE "FAITH FUND."
AS WORD GOT OUT ABOUT THE FAITH FUND, OTHERS BEGAN TO GIVE TOWARDS SAMUEL'S EDUCATION.

SAMUEL VISITED AN AFRICAN AMERICAN CHURCH IN FORT WAYNE HIS FIRST SUNDAY. THE CHURCH WAS A DISTANCE FROM TAYLOR AND HE ARRIVED LATE.
HE INTRODUCED HIMSELF AND SAID THAT HE HAD A MESSAGE FOR THE CHURCH.
THE MINISTER WAS RELUCTANT AT FIRST BUT THEN SAW THE GLOW OF GOD IN SAMUEL AND AGREED.
EVERYONE IN THE CHURCH FELL TO THEIR KNEES, SOME WEEPING AND OTHERS REJOICING OVER WHAT GOD WAS DOING AMONG THEM.
HE RECALLED LATER THAT HE DID NOT REMEMBER ANYTHING SAMUEL SAID, BUT HE DID REMEMBER THE PRESENCE OF GOD IN THE ROOM.
FORT WAYNE
THE REVIVAL WAS COVERED IN THE NEWSPAPERS, AND THE NAME OF THE YOUNG AFRICAN MAN STUDYING AT TAYLOR BECAME WIDELY KNOWN.
PEOPLE TRAVELED TO FORT WAYNE JUST TO MEET SAMUEL, AND HE HANDED EACH PERSON A BIBLE AND ASKED THEM TO READ SOME VERSES OUT LOUD.
AS PEOPLE READ SAMUEL HID GOD'S WORD IN HIS HEART.

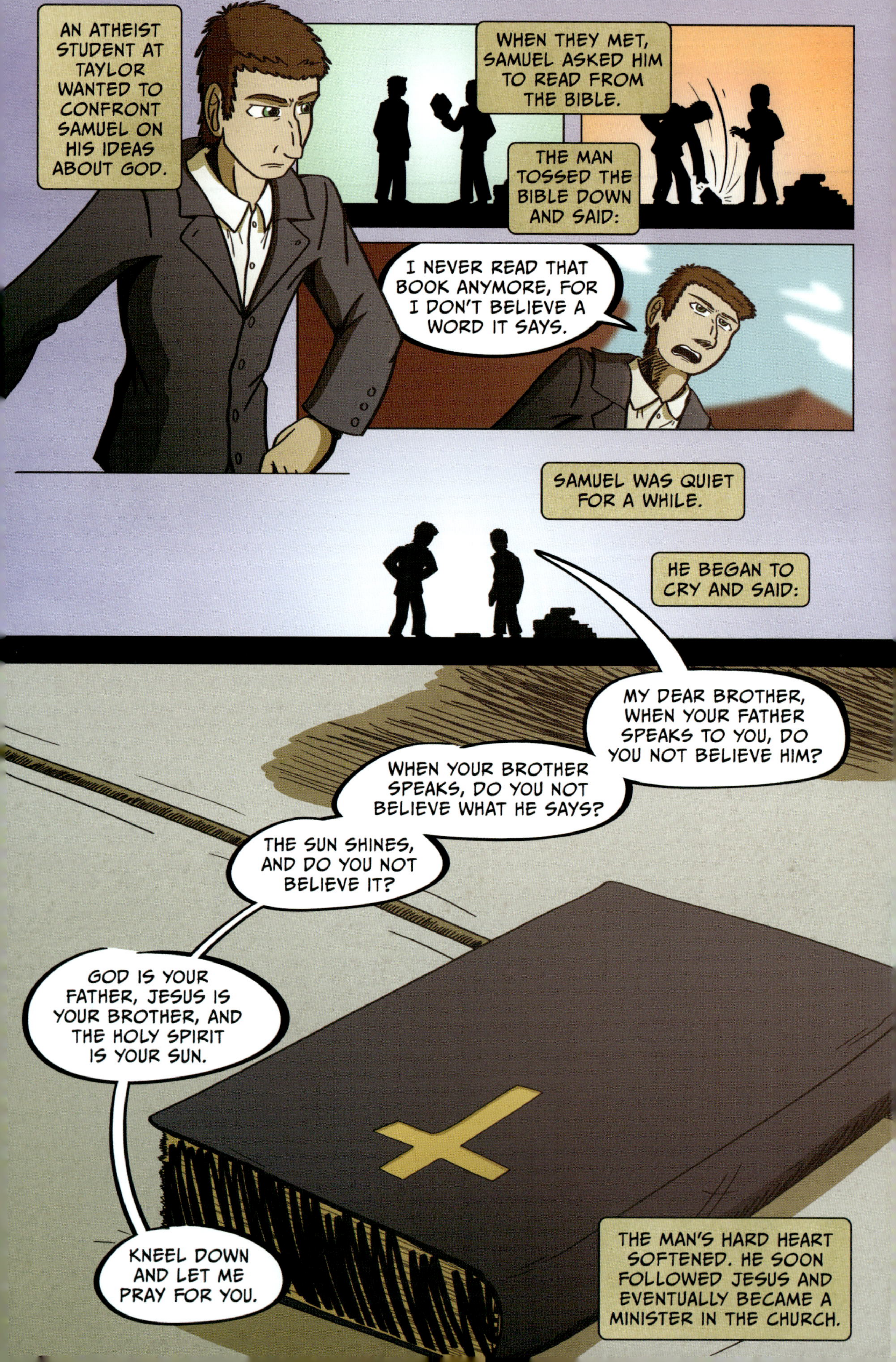
AN ATHEIST STUDENT AT TAYLOR WANTED TO CONFRONT SAMUEL ON HIS IDEAS ABOUT GOD.
WHEN THEY MET, SAMUEL ASKED HIM TO READ FROM THE BIBLE.
THE MAN TOSSED THE BIBLE DOWN AND SAID:
I NEVER READ THAT BOOK ANYMORE, FOR I DON'T BELIEVE A WORD IT SAYS.
SAMUEL WAS QUIET FOR A WHILE.
HE BEGAN TO CRY AND SAID:
MY DEAR BROTHER, WHEN YOUR FATHER SPEAKS TO YOU, DO YOU NOT BELIEVE HIM?
WHEN YOUR BROTHER SPEAKS, DO YOU NOT BELIEVE WHAT HE SAYS?
THE SUN SHINES, AND DO YOU NOT BELIEVE IT?
GOD IS YOUR FATHER, JESUS IS YOUR BROTHER, AND THE HOLY SPIRIT IS YOUR SUN.
KNEEL DOWN AND LET ME PRAY FOR YOU.
THE MAN'S HARD HEART SOFTENED. HE SOON FOLLOWED JESUS AND EVENTUALLY BECAME A MINISTER IN THE CHURCH.

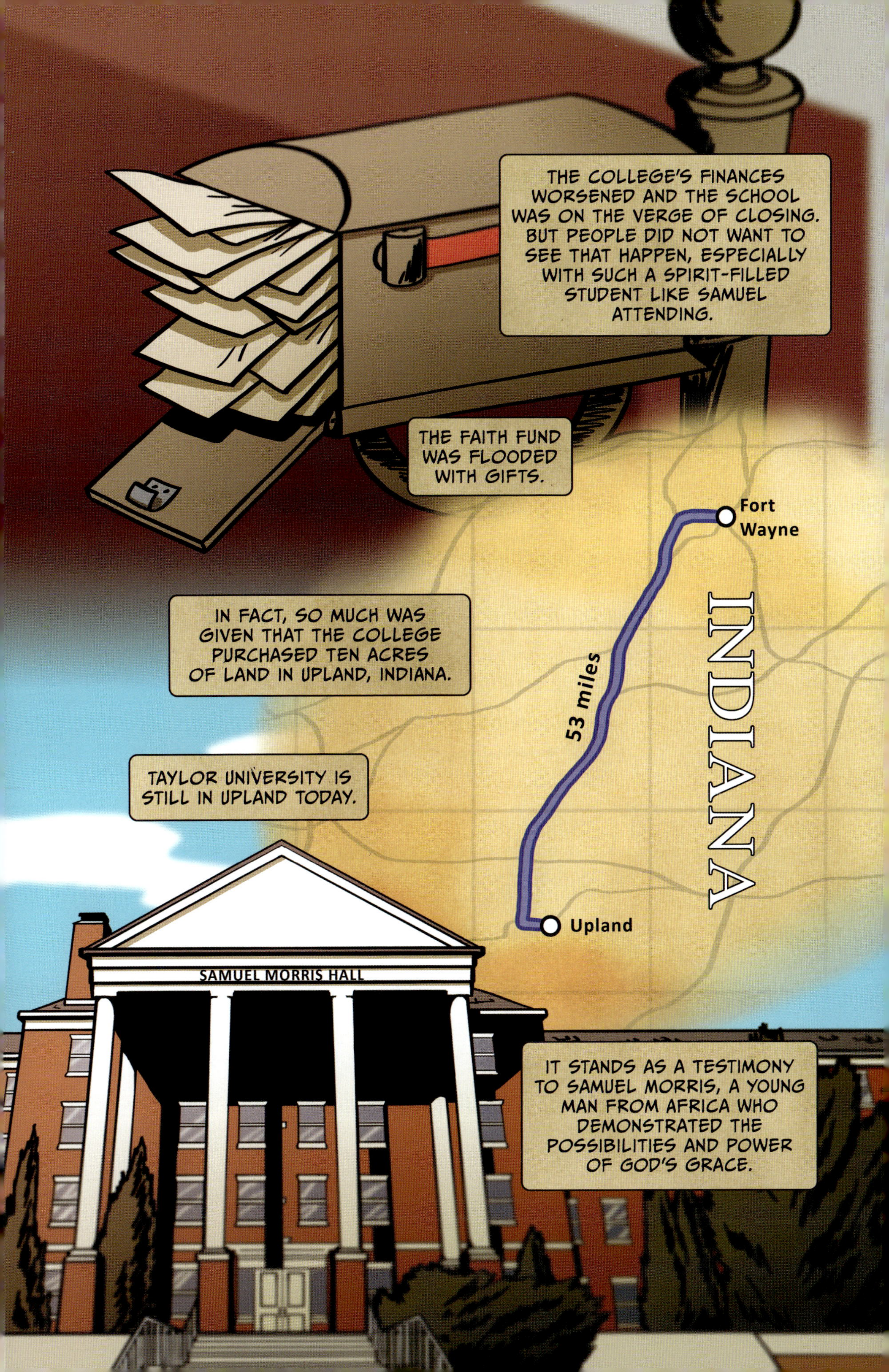
THE COLLEGE'S FINANCES WORSENED AND THE SCHOOL WAS ON THE VERGE OF CLOSING. BUT PEOPLE DID NOT WANT TO SEE THAT HAPPEN, ESPECIALLY WITH SUCH A SPIRIT-FILLED STUDENT LIKE SAMUEL ATTENDING.
THE FAITH FUND WAS FLOODED WITH GIFTS.
IN FACT, SO MUCH WAS GIVEN THAT THE COLLEGE PURCHASED TEN ACRES OF LAND IN UPLAND, INDIANA.
Fort Wayne
53 miles
INDIANA
Upland
TAYLOR UNIVERSITY IS STILL IN UPLAND TODAY.
SAMUEL MORRIS HALL
IT STANDS AS A TESTIMONY TO SAMUEL MORRIS, A YOUNG MAN FROM AFRICA WHO DEMONSTRATED THE POSSIBILITIES AND POWER OF GOD'S GRACE.

SAMUEL LOVED HIS LIFE IN AMERICA. THE CHANGE OF SEASONS INSPIRED HIM,
BUT THE WINTERS PROVED TOO MUCH FOR THIS YOUNG MAN FROM THE TROPICS OF AFRICA.
A SEVERE COLD GREW WORSE.
THOUGH HE ATTENDED CLASSES AND CHURCH SERVICES, HE WAS VERY ILL. HE WAS TAKEN TO A HOSPITAL IN FORT WAYNE TO RECEIVE CARE, BUT NEVER RECOVERED.
SAMUEL STRUGGLED WITH HIS LACK OF HEALING AT FIRST. THEN GOD REVEALED THAT HE WOULD SOON BE IN THE PLACE WHERE "THE INHABITANT SHALL NOT SAY, I AM SICK."
HE DIED IN MAY 1893.
SAMUEL MORRIS NEVER RETURNED TO AFRICA, BUT OTHERS WERE CALLED TO GO IN HIS PLACE. AT A PRAYER MEETING AFTER HIS PASSING, THREE PEOPLE COMMITTED THEMSELVES TO THE WORK.
ONE YOUNG MAN SAID, "I MUST GO TO AFRICA IN HIS PLACE. IT IS MY PRAYER THAT THE MANTLE OF HIS SIMPLE FAITH WILL BE THROWN OVER ME."
TO THOSE WHO MIGHT DOUBT THE REMARKABLE LIFE OF SAMUEL MORRIS, LET THEM CONSIDER THESE WORDS FROM DR. READE:
"MOST OF US HAVE GONE TOO FAR AWAY FROM THE SIMPLE FAITH OF CHILDHOOD, AND GOD CANNOT DO MANY MIGHTY WORKS IN US BECAUSE OF OUR UNBELIEF."